Meditation Is an Open Sky

To all of my mindfulness teachers,
with infinite gratitude, WS

For Ardian and Felix,
I'll eat you up, I love you so! SR

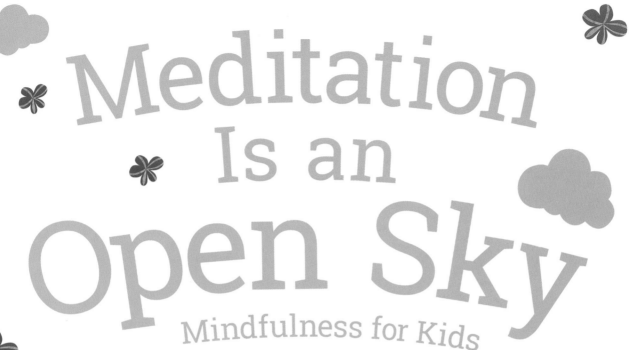

Meditation Is an Open Sky

Mindfulness for Kids

Whitney Stewart

pictures by
Sally Rippin

Albert Whitman & Company
Chicago, Illinois

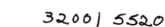

Contents

You know when you're having a bad day and nothing seems to go right? You have that WOBBLY feeling inside that makes you scared, sad, and mad all at the same time.

HUMPF

Well, find a quiet place, sit down, and **MEDITATE**.

GRRRRRRR

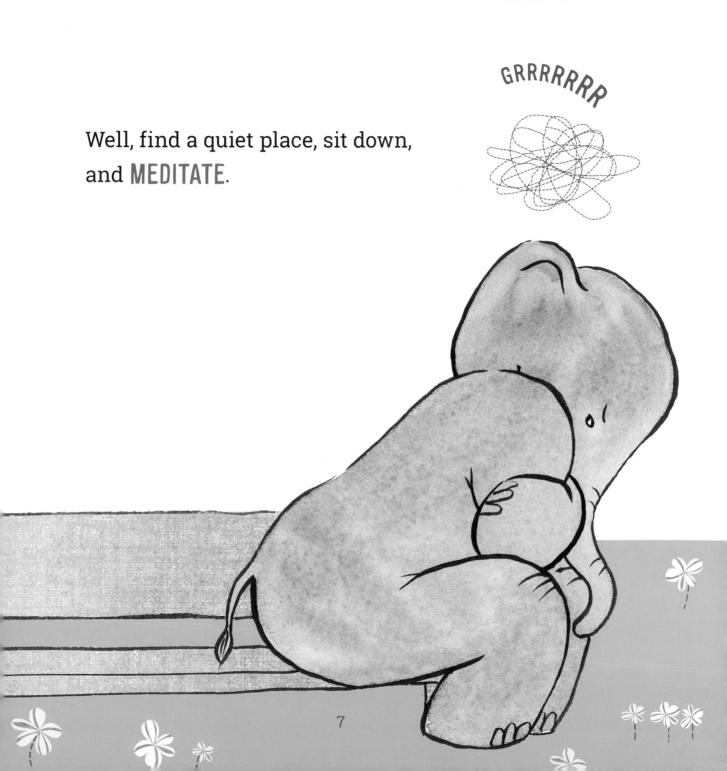

7

Meditation won't take away your problems, but it will help you deal with them. You'll learn to watch your feelings pop up and disappear like soap bubbles.

8

Read through this book and pick one meditation
for today.

Sit in a chair or cross-legged on a pillow on the floor.

Keep your back straight but not stiff and put your hands
on your knees or in your lap.

Close your eyes or keep them slightly open and stare
at a spot on the floor.

Inhale and feel your breath fill up your belly.

Then breathe out slowly. Continue with slow, full breaths
during meditation.

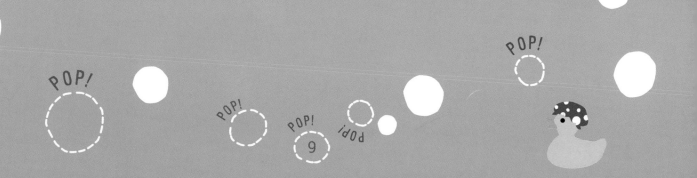

POP!

POP!

POP!

POP!

POP!

9

Mind Drawing

for

Focus

Practice this meditation to help you concentrate and think clearly.

Think of an object that makes you happy. It can be as simple as a flower or as complicated as a castle. Now draw it in your mind. Add details and color.

If your mind wanders, pretend your thoughts are bubbles and  them. Go back to your drawing.

When your drawing is done, look at it with your mind. Enjoy it for five or ten minutes. When you're ready, breathe in and out deeply and get up slowly. Carry your calm mind with you.

Protection Circle
for
Security

Sometimes you feel scared, and you
want to relax and feel protected.

Imagine a glowing ball of white light between your eyebrows. Breathe out and send the light out of your forehead to surround your body. You're sitting in a circle of white light, and it makes you safe.

Now you have a ball of red light inside your throat. Breathe out, and the red light streams all around your body. You're doubly safe in rings of white and red light.

Finally, imagine blue light inside your heart. Breathe out and send the blue light around your body. Feel protected inside three circles of light—WHITE, **RED**, and BLUE.

Stay in the light for several minutes and get up slowly. Take that safe feeling with you.

Jigsaw Puzzle
for
 Wisdom

If you're feeling all mixed up, try this
meditation to see your true self.

Close your eyes and imagine you're a jigsaw puzzle, made up
of hundreds of pieces. These pieces are feelings, moods, and
thoughts that change minute by minute. Take a few pieces
away and ask yourself, **"AM I STILL THERE?"**

Imagine the puzzle falling apart into a heap on the ground.
Where are you now? Your inner wisdom is there even when
your pieces are scattered.

Use your wisdom mind and put the jigsaw puzzle back
together. When you are whole again, breathe in and out
deeply. Your inner wisdom is always with you.

Special Place
for
Relaxation

Try this meditation when you're
fidgety and can't settle down.

Imagine taking a trip to the beach, the mountains, or a grassy park. Any place you're happy. What do you see? What do you smell? What do you hear? How is the weather? Are you by yourself or with friends? Run around and play or sleep under a tree.

This is your SPECIAL place, and nobody can disturb you here.

Before you leave, you find a present. It's a gift from your inner wisdom. It will always be here, in your special place, waiting for you to return.

Friendship Meditation
for
☁ Kindness ☁

Practice this one when
someone you know needs joy.

Think of someone kind. Someone you know or an imaginary person. You feel happy when this person hugs you or says something nice.

Imagine that happy feeling as a pulsing white light in your heart. Send that light from your heart to someone else's heart. See that person feel better.

Now send your white light to everyone in the world. They are all smiling and bubbling with joy. Feel that goodness. Sit with it for five or ten minutes. Take it with you when you open your eyes and stand up.

Send that heart light even when you're not meditating.

Mind Clearing

for
Clarity

Sometimes you want to clear your
mind of troubling thoughts.

Imagine a glowing ball of white light at the top of your head. It has the power to clear your bad moods, hurt feelings, and worries. See it expand and pour down into you. Now see your ugly feelings turn into gray smoke. As white light fills you up, it pushes the gray smoke out of your mouth, nose, and ears. Then the smoke vanishes into the air. Sit with this fresh feeling inside you. For five minutes or ten.

Feel LIGHTER when you finish your meditation.

Wise Friend

for

Decision-Making

Sometimes you can't make up your
mind and need guidance.

When you're stuck and don't know what to do, imagine
sitting next to a wise friend who sends white light into
your forehead to strengthen your body. Then the wise
one sends red light into your throat to
help you speak clearly and
blue light into your
heart to settle
your mind.

Now ask your friend what to do and listen to the answer.
Make sure it's the right answer and thank your friend.

See yourself following this advice and solving your problem.
Feel relief from making the right choice.

Now ask yourself, "Where did that wisdom come from?"

You know the answer. That wisdom is always inside you.
You are your own wise friend.

Bursting Emotion

for 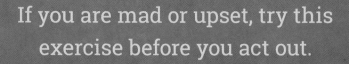 Control

If you are mad or upset, try this
exercise before you act out.

If you're angry, hurt, or sad, don't say anything right away.
Sit down and breathe slowly, counting up to ten. Let your
in-breath fill your belly and your out-breath tickle your
nostrils. When you reach ten, start counting again.

Notice how your body feels. Is your heart racing? Is your
stomach tight? Breathe into the place in your body where
the anger or hurt goes. If your mind starts telling you a
story about what made you upset, don't listen right now.

Just watch the sensations in your body and breathe.

Whatever feelings you have, don't fight them. They will soften and fade away as you pay attention to your body sensations. Keep breathing until you find a settled place inside yourself. Then sit for a few minutes longer.

Be gentle with yourself.

Big Sky Mind

for

 Openness

Life feels overwhelming sometimes,
and you want calmness.

Find a place where you can lie on the ground and stare up
at the sky. Feel your breath come in and go out. If you see
clouds, watch them change shapes and move across the
sky, just like your thoughts across your mind. If you
think of a problem, focus on the sky again.
Breathe slowly and deeply.
Stay there as long
as you can.

Let your mind be as wide and open as the sky.

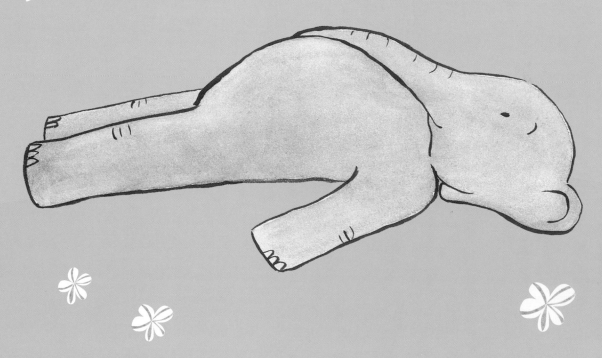

What do I do when I feel...?

1 **Bored**

Your mind might hop around from one thought to the next. It has a hard time keeping quiet. You don't have to fix it. Start by meditating in short spurts. Then add a few minutes each time.

2 **Wriggly**

Try a silent walking meditation and focus on your feet as you walk. Breathe and step. Breathe and step, for ten minutes.

3 **Sore legs**

If your feet go to sleep or your legs hurt, use an extra pillow under your bottom or try meditating in a chair, with your feet firmly planted on the ground.

When something hurts, notice the discomfort for a second before you move. This increases your inner awareness. You can also do a sitting meditation for a few minutes and then a walking meditation.

4 Sleepy

If you get sleepy, try opening your eyes and staring at the floor. If that doesn't work, shift your gaze higher and take full breaths. Or take a nap, then meditate.

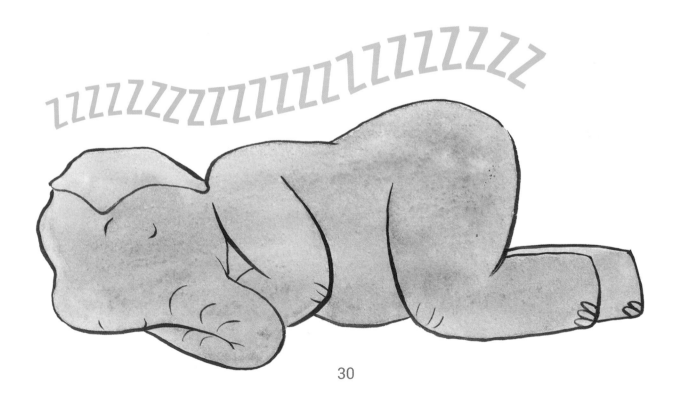

5 Scared

If you feel scared, notice where your fear goes and breathe into that part of your body. If that doesn't help, try chanting a pleasant word like "BLUEBIRD, BLUEBIRD, BLUEBIRD" or sing a special song. If you're still scared, talk to an adult you trust. You might have a good reason for your fear, and you might need help. Ask for it.

6 Frustrated

Meditation has nothing to do with being bad or good, right or wrong. That's your mind babbling. Just sit and breathe. If your mind wanders, bring it back to full attention. You are learning to work with your mind. Each meditation session is different because no minute is exactly like the next. Have no expectations and be kind to yourself.

Library of Congress Cataloging-in-Publication Data is on file with the publisher.

Text copyright © 2014 by Whitney Stewart
Illustrations copyright © 2014 Sally Rippin
First published in 2014 as *Big Sky Mind*
by Windy Hollow Books, Melbourne, Australia.
Published in 2015 by Albert Whitman & Company
ISBN 978-0-8075-4908-7

Printed in China.
10 9 8 7 6 5 4 3 2 1 HH 20 19 18 17 16 15 14

The design is by Regine Abos and Ellen Kokontis.

For more information about Albert Whitman & Company,
visit our web site at www.albertwhitman.com.